BEI GRIN MACHT SICH IHR WISSEN BEZAHLT

- Wir veröffentlichen Ihre Hausarbeit,
  Bachelor- und Masterarbeit

- Ihr eigenes eBook und Buch -
  weltweit in allen wichtigen Shops

- Verdienen Sie an jedem Verkauf

Jetzt bei www.GRIN.com hochladen und kostenlos publizieren

Bibliografische Information der Deutschen Nationalbibliothek:

Die Deutsche Bibliothek verzeichnet diese Publikation in der Deutschen National-
bibliografie; detaillierte bibliografische Daten sind im Internet über http://dnb.d-
nb.de/ abrufbar.

Dieses Werk sowie alle darin enthaltenen einzelnen Beiträge und Abbildungen
sind urheberrechtlich geschützt. Jede Verwertung, die nicht ausdrücklich vom
Urheberrechtsschutz zugelassen ist, bedarf der vorherigen Zustimmung des Verla-
ges. Das gilt insbesondere für Vervielfältigungen, Bearbeitungen, Übersetzungen,
Mikroverfilmungen, Auswertungen durch Datenbanken und für die Einspeicherung
und Verarbeitung in elektronische Systeme. Alle Rechte, auch die des auszugsweisen
Nachdrucks, der fotomechanischen Wiedergabe (einschließlich Mikrokopie) sowie
der Auswertung durch Datenbanken oder ähnliche Einrichtungen, vorbehalten.

Impressum:

Copyright © 2010 GRIN Verlag, Open Publishing GmbH
Druck und Bindung: Books on Demand GmbH, Norderstedt Germany
ISBN: 9783656446866

Serge Ajamian

Globalization, Democracy, and outcomes of Internationalization

GRIN Verlag

GRIN - Your knowledge has value

Der GRIN Verlag publiziert seit 1998 wissenschaftliche Arbeiten von Studenten, Hochschullehrern und anderen Akademikern als eBook und gedrucktes Buch. Die Verlagswebsite www.grin.com ist die ideale Plattform zur Veröffentlichung von Hausarbeiten, Abschlussarbeiten, wissenschaftlichen Aufsätzen, Dissertationen und Fachbüchern.

Besuchen Sie uns im Internet:

http://www.grin.com/

http://www.facebook.com/grincom

http://www.twitter.com/grin_com

Globalization, Democracy, and outcomes of Internationalization

Globalization and the Spread of Democracy:

In the post-cold War political discourse, the notion of democracy has been the spearhead in the American foreign policy agenda. For many of the Washington based think tanks, globalization through its corporate, economic, monetary, technological, and cultural elements has been the primary assertion of policies to promote democracy and liberal economic ideals throughout the world, hence establishing and imposing a post Cold War Pax- Americana through political and economic hegemony. However, to better understand this intertwined relationship between globalization and democracy it is important to breakdown the dynamics of liberal economics and political capitalism in parallels with the enforcement of the international market system.

Globalization, "described as the increasing global integration of economies, information technology, the spread of global popular culture, and other forms of human interaction", (Lieber and Weisberg 274) has been an unprecedented force in our modern history and has influenced and shaped new economic and political trends throughout the world with the defeat of the Soviet Union and the establishment of multi-polar world that replaced a bi-polar Soviet versus Western block and has brought new meaning in the function of an internationally oriented market in the perception of today's political ideology and economics. According to Sanjoy Chakravorty, author of *Urban Development in the global periphery: The consequences of economic and ideological Globalization*, globalization in reality have two essential elements. First Chakravorty refers to the notion of economic globalization as part of the "integration of global markets". (Chakravorty 357) According to Chakravorty, "economic globalization, whether measured by trade or capital flows, is primarily a First World phenomenon; and just as significant, this is increasingly true. "Economic globalization has successfully been achieved in integrating the world through the establishment of an economic symbiosis between different regions and parts of the world. On the other hand, globalization can also been described as an ideological forces that refers to the political ideas that underlie the spread of markets, trade, and democracy." (Chakravorty 357) Ultimately, these ideological tools manifested in the creation of internationalized institutions such as the World Bank and the International Monetary Fund largely supported via capital flows from the United States and the West. Conditions set by the institutions often insisted on economic and political reforms as an incentive for funding for projects, ultimately influencing democratic changes in an LDC given its underperforming economy. According to Samuel Huntington, a prominent contemporary political scholar and author of *The Third Wave of Democratization*, "In the 1990s the International Monetary Fund (IIMF) and the World Bank conceivably become much more forceful than they have heretofore been in making political democratization as well as economic liberalization a precondition for economic assistance."(Huntington 8)

In a further breakdown of the constituents of economic globalization spread by Western sponsored international institutions and its correlation to democracy, social spending policies channeled through World Bank and IMF funds and socio-economic reforms are considered to be pivotal in the push of the democratic progress in developing or less developed nations. According to Nita Rudra, author of *Globalization and the Strengthening of Democracy in the Developing World*,

> "An interesting pattern emerges from the results. Openness in both trade and capital markets has a robust and indirect effect on democratization via social spending. Capital flows, like trade, demonstrate a positive relationship with democracy if and only if increases in social spending accompany increasing levels of globalization. In other words, as trade and financial market integration deepens, significant levels of welfare spending are required before democracy improves." (Rudra 706)

In its relationship to democracy and how the these ideological and economic globalization forces have influenced winds for democracy throughout the world, it has been widely suggested that globalization is merely but a tool to effectively establish an American economic, political, and cultural hegemony throughout the world through the export of an internationalized dynamic for economic integration and political interaction accompanied by cultural undertones. In effect, the very values of democracy i.e. liberty, freedom amplified by the United States are merely the façade behind America's agenda on domination and control. In fact, President Bill Clinton, shortly before the end of his presidency was cited saying, "In the new century, liberty will be spread by cell phone and cable modem."(Lieber and Weisberg 274)

In Huntington's analysis of the democratization process in the world, he asserts the cultural variable in determining whether a country can pass the democracy litmus test. Huntington attests that "the world's great historic cultural traditions vary significantly in the extent to which their attitudes, values, beliefs, and related behavior patterns are conducive to the development of democracy." (Huntington 13) Globalization, in fact, can be considered the international manifestation as the end product of the "Western Christianity's" progress from feudalism, the Renaissance, the Reformation, the Enlightenment, the French Revolution, and eventually liberalism referred to by Samuel Huntington as the "Western-culture thesis".(13)

Emerging from this discourse, scholars seem to be split on whether globalization has actually reinforced democratic ideals in the world. One particular school of thought considers globalization as a set of aggressive cultural, economic, and political forces that have set the platform for inter-state interaction and the basis of their success in the international arena. (Chakravorty 358) Supporters of this school of thought claim that globalization has marginalized the individualistic culture and identity of states as they have become prone to globalization's "homogenizing process, an economic and cultural assault led by the American juggernauts of Coca colonization and McDonaldization...where many have gone so far as to suggest that in order to succeed in the global economy there are certain universal "cultural imperatives" that cities must follow." (Chakravorty 358) Aligned with this school of thought, it is also believed by many that globalization has in fact not been successful in promoting positive democratic reform pattern, rather becoming more of a destructive force for these very democratic institutions for countries on their path to democratization where the actual global process "seems to undermine the nation-state as well as liberal democracy." (Gorg and Hirsch 585) Authors Gorg and Hirsch harshly criticize the role played by international institutions and the creation of the "international democracy". The concept of international democracy, to many, is embedded within the realm of international control and hegemony of the haves against the have-nots in this case meaning the rich developed countries versus less developed, underdeveloped, and developing societies. In fact, John Perkins, author of Confessions of en economic Hit man, speaks of the role played by the international corporatocracy where he describes his experiences in his career as an EHM or an economic hit man, during the period where he worked as a consultant for an American engineering firm MAIN. According to Perkins,

> "EHMs are highly paid professionals who cheat countries around the globe out of trillions of dollars. They funnel money from the World Bank, the U.S. Agency for International Development USAID, and other foreign aid organisations into the coffers of huge corporations...Their tools include fraudulent financial reports, rigged elections, payoffs, extortion, sex, and murder. They play a game as old as an empire, but one that has taken on new and terrifying dimensions during this time of globalization" (Perkins 20)

Given the ambiguous role of these international institutions there seems to be a hidden agenda behind political and economic reforms in return for financial incentive and has many such as Christophe Gorg and Joachim Hirsch, authors of *Is international democracy possible?*, assess the detriments caused through the globalization process on the individualistic democratic features of nations states. Gorg and Hirsch attest that "globalization process constitutes a threat to 'democracy' by restricting the political scope of individual states is based on the close connection between liberal democracy and capitalist nation-states. (587) The article clearly delineates the reasons behind the disintegration of the democratic process in nation states die to globalization. First, globalization has been focused on enhancing the "international dimension" that requires the importance of political regulations that are far beyond the decision-making jurisdiction of these states where the focus has been primarily on instituting universal standards and regulations through "the increased significance of international and supra-national organizations" (587) Second reason has been the deregulation of capital and financial markets that have "reduce the capacity of nation-states, notably in regard to economic and social policies. This will necessarily bring about a 'hollowing out' of both democratic institutions and procedures, making them increasingly futile." (587) Finally, the authors emphasize on the role played by the non-state actors such as the NGOs and multi-national corporatocracy as more darkly described by John Perkins in the *Confessions of An Economic Hit Man.* According to Gorg and Hirsch, "there is an ever growing number of NGOs (non-governmental organizations) which are varied in their goals and their significance, and which exist not only alongside but also in competition with state organizations." (587)

In conclusion, one cannot ignore the great strands that globalization has contributed to development of human society and the detriments it has caused to what it initially promoted, democracy. As Nita Rudra stated, trade and capital flows provided through the mechanisms of globalization coupled with "increasing exposure to international export and financial markets leads to improvements in democracy if safety nets are used simultaneously as a strategy for providing stability and building political support" (Rudra 706) At the same time, globalization also promotes difference and plurality of cultural values and political "formations of identity, generating resistance that is empowered and liberating." (Chakravorty 357)

References:

Chakravorty S. "Urban development in the global periphery: The consequences of economic and ideological globalization." Annals of Regional Science. 37 (3):357-367. 2003

Görg C. and Joachim H, "Is International Democracy Possible?" Taylor and Francis Ltd. 5 (4):585-615 1998

Huntington, Samuel. "Democracy's Third Wave". University of Oklahoma Press, 1991

Perkins, John. "Confessions of an Economic Hit Man." Berrett-Koehler Publishers, 2004

Rudra, N. "Globalization and the Strengthening of Democracy in the Developing World." Midwest Political Science Association 49 (4): 704-730

Lieber, Robert and Weisberg, Ruth. "Globalization, Culture, and Identities in Crisis" International Journal of Politics, Culture and Society, Vol. 16, No. 2, Winter 2002